All About Animals
Rhinoceroses

By Justine Ciovacco

Reader's Digest Young Families

Contents

Chapter 1
A Rhinoceros Grows Up

So Much Milk

Rhino calves drink an amount of milk equal to 20 full glasses each day.

It is just another hot, dry afternoon for everyone on the African plain except one female white rhinoceros. She had been lying near a shallow pool of water with other female rhinos. Now she slowly walks away from the group to a part of the grassland that seems quiet and safe. It has been nearly one and a half years—517 days to be exact—since she first became pregnant, and she is almost ready to give birth.

The mother-to-be spends a few days waiting alone. Then she gives birth to one calf. Mama Rhinoceros cleans her new son with soft, firm licks. She stands over him and watches every move he makes.

Baby Rhinoceros can stand up within an hour after he is born. Soon he tucks his head under his mother's belly and drinks her warm milk. He needs milk to grow and be strong. A few hours later, he's ready to go for a walk.

Big Baby

A newborn white rhinoceros weighs 110 pounds at birth. That's about as heavy as 15 human babies!

For the next few weeks, Baby Rhinoceros and his mother stay by themselves while Baby Rhino grows. Sometimes they walk through the dry grassland side by side, but often Mama walks a few steps ahead to better protect her little one against sudden danger. The biggest dangers are lions and tigers who hunt rhino calves, but they are rarely a match for a mother rhinoceros.

Baby Rhino chomps on patches of grass and other plants, just like his mother. Every few hours he drinks milk. When Mama Rhinoceros thinks her son is ready to meet other rhinos, she nudges him into areas where there are rhinos she knows. But if they or other animals get too close to her calf, Mama Rhinoceros quickly steps between them.

When Baby Rhinoceros is five weeks old, his horns begin to grow above his nostrils. He and his mama spend most of their day with a small group of rhinos. Mama lets him play with the other calves. She and Baby Rhinoceros often mew softly to let each other know they are nearby.

Wild Words
A female rhinoceros is called a **cow**. *A male rhino is a* **bull**. *Their baby is called a* **calf**.

Daddy Time

By age 10, a male rhinoceros is ready to father his own calf.

For the next two years, Baby Rhinoceros stays with his mother. He continues to drink her milk and rest near her in the sun. She still tries to protect him from predators.

Baby Rhinoceros knows it's time to leave his mother's side when she is pregnant with a new calf. He wanders farther and farther from her each day until she is ready to give birth. He likes spending more time by himself. Soon he decides he wants his own piece of land.

Baby Rhinoceros walks far enough away to find land that doesn't smell like the urine or dung of other rhinos. When he finds the perfect spot, he sprays his urine all around. Then he makes large piles of dung and stomps on them with his thick feet. Finally, he walks around his territory so he can spread the dung on the land. Now all rhinos can smell that this area is his. He has made his own home sweet home!

One Smell Can Tell

Female rhinoceroses walk anywhere they want. Males can too, but they can't stay too long in areas that smell like other male rhinos. A male rhinoceros marks his territory with urine and dung to let other rhinos know he owns the place.

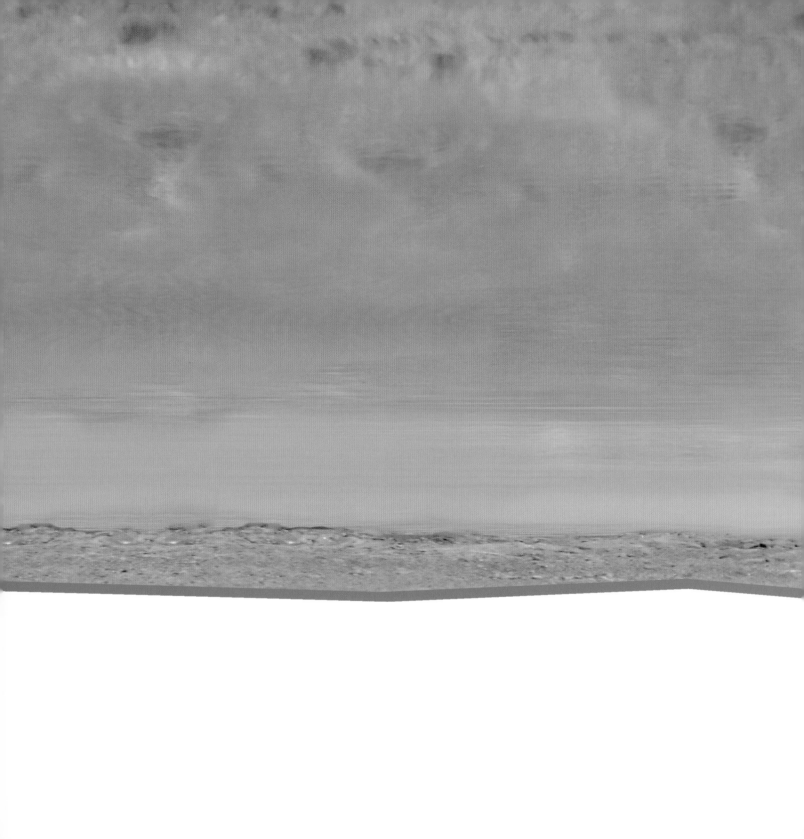

Chapter 2
The Body of a Rhinoceros

On Tiptoe!

Rhinoceroses walk and run on tiptoe! They have three toes on each foot, which is protected by a thick hoof.

Rhinoceroses are the third largest mammals on Earth. Only hippopotamuses and elephants are larger.

Big Bodies

The first thing you notice about a rhinoceros is how big and blocky it is. It is tall, up to 6 feet high (about the height of a basketball player). It is wide. And it is very, very heavy—up to 3 tons!

Rhinoceroses have tough, thick skin. Their skin protects them from sharp twigs and thorns that could scratch them as they walk through tall grass and between bushes and trees.

Most rhinoceroses look hairless, but they are not. A rhinoceros has hair on its ears and the end of its tail. It also has eyelashes.

Surprisingly Swift

Despite their large size, rhinoceroses can run as fast as 30 miles an hour for short distances. That's about the speed of a car on a city street. Like their horse relatives, rhinos gallop high on their toes. This position helps to give them speed.

Five of a Kind

There are five species (kinds) of rhinoceroses. The biggest is the white rhinoceros. It isn't really white, just like the black rhinoceros isn't black. Both are shades of gray and live in Africa.

The other three kinds of rhinos live in Southeast Asia. Javan and Indian rhinoceroses look like they are wearing suits of armor. They have stiff, thick folds of skin over their shoulders and rear end. The skin is more flexible on the folded areas, helping the rhinos to move more easily. The Indian rhinoceros also has bumps on its skin.

The smallest rhino is the Sumatran rhinoceros. It is sometimes called "the hairy rhinoceros." Young Sumatran rhinos have patches of shaggy, stiff reddish-brown hair on their backs and sides, and darker, thick hair on the tips of their ears. As they grow older, their hair turns darker and sometimes falls off.

Color Change

This white rhinoceros shows how rhino skin color can change as the animal grows older. Part of the color change depends on how much time the rhinoceros has spent wallowing in mud or dirt.

The skin of Indian rhinoceroses looks like the suits of armor worn by medieval knights. They are the only rhinoceroses with bumps on their skin.

The horns of rhinoceroses are so thick, sharp, and strong that some can cut through metal!

Heavy Horns

The word *rhinoceros* comes from two Greek words that mean "nose horn." All rhinoceroses have at least one horn on the top of their nose. White, black, and Sumatran rhinoceroses have two horns. The horn at the front of the nose is usually larger than the one behind it.

A rhinoceros's horn is made of the same tough material as your nails. It is called keratin. But the keratin in rhino horns forms layers and becomes thick and solid.

Rhinoceroses use their horns to jab other rhinos that get too close. Rhinos are rougher with their horns when they fight. The horns are also helpful in pulling down tall bushes and tree branches so the rhinos can reach the leaves. Sometimes rhinos dig up dirt with their horns. Scientists think they are looking for salt, water, or food.

Rhinoceroses are not born with horns. Horns start to grow in when the calves are about 5 weeks old. Unlike deer horns, rhino horns grow out of the animal's skin and not their bones. Once a horn grows in, it never stops growing! It grows about 3 to 8 inches longer each year. If a horn breaks off, it grows back.

Humongous Horn

The horn of a white rhino can be 5 feet long. That's taller than you are now!

Rhinoceros Senses

A rhinoceros's eyes are tiny and are on either side of its head. This position makes it hard to see things straight ahead. The rhino must turn its head from side to side and look out one eye at a time. As a result, a rhinoceros can't see very well, which is why it sometimes runs into objects that don't move, such as trees and rocks.

However, rhinoceroses have an excellent sense of smell. Their big nostrils can pick up scents as far as eight football fields away! Mothers and calves know each others' scents, which helps them stay close. The scent of a predator causes rhinos to move away quickly. A good sense of smell also helps them figure out if a male rhino has marked a territory as his own as they wander through it.

The ears of a rhinoceros are on top of its head. This helps it hear sounds from far away. A rhino can turn its ears to hear sounds from different directions.

Tales of the Tail

A rhino's tail is short with stiff hairs that hang down at the end. It makes an excellent flyswatter! If a rhino is scared, it sometimes curls its tail into a corkscrew shape.

A rhinoceros's thick, straight legs help to support the animal's massive size and weight. But they make the process of lying down awkward. A rhino bends its back legs into a slight kneel and then lowers the rest of its body until it is laying down in a heap.

Myth Maker

Some people think the myth of the unicorn might have been based on a type of rhinoceros that lived thousands of years ago in southern Russia and the Ukraine. It was a long, tall animal with a 7-foot-long horn that grew out of its forehead. This rhinoceros species is called *Elasmotherium*.

Chapter 3
Rhinoceros Life

Rhino Rubs

Rhinoceroses like to rub their big bodies against trees and bushes as a way to scratch their itches. Rubbing also leaves a rhino's scent behind. The scent is like a sign saying, "I have been here and may come back!"

Rolling in mud and dirt helps rhinoceroses to protect their skin from the sun and insect bites. It is also a great way to cool off on a hot day.

All in a Day

Most rhinoceroses live alone but near other rhinos. They usually share the places where they eat, drink water, and wallow in mud. White rhinoceroses are the only ones that form groups. The groups are small—only up to six animals. White rhinos spend a few hours together each day as they eat or search for water.

Rhinoceroses graze most of the day and take rest breaks. Black and white rhinos in Africa may not eat much until after the sun goes down. They can sleep standing up, but they often try to lie down in a shady area.

Indian rhinoceroses are good swimmers. They live in swampy jungle areas and bathe every day. When the sun is out, they cool off in a river and eat the plants growing there. These rhinos push their way through the jungle plants to get to water. This helps other animals that follow the paths to water.

Javan rhinos are also good swimmers. They have even been seen swimming in the Indian Ocean!

Big Swimmers

Indian rhinoceroses spend more than half of every day wallowing in mud to keep cool. They are great swimmers. They can even dive and eat under water!

Picking a Fight

Rhinoceroses are so big that people assume they must also be tough. But rhinos don't like to fight. If left alone, rhinoceroses will usually not attack.

Black rhinoceroses are the most likely to fight. If they smell anything unusual, they charge forward. This reaction has scared many humans trying to get a closer look!

Rhinoceroses sometimes fight with each other. Males battle for a female or to take over a piece of land. Male and female rhinos sometimes fight when they first meet each other. The female may not like the male's way of giving her attention and may attack to make him stay away. It rarely works for long.

Ready, Set, Charge!

When a young rhino play-fights, it learns the basics of attacking — but without hurting the other rhino. As an adult, an attacking rhino first lowers its head and may snort. Then it races forward up to a speed of 30 miles an hour. A galloping rhino can cause serious damage, even death.

Female rhinoceroses use their horns to charge at predators that come near their children.

When it wants to show it is in charge, a rhinoceros may go horn to horn with another rhinoceros and make a low growl.

Sound Off

Rhinoceroses make many sounds to communicate with one another. Males and females whistle and snort to get the other's attention. Rhinos in a fight may grunt or scream. Rhinoceroses that are upset sometimes squeal or growl.

Black rhinoceroses make the most sounds of all rhinos. The babies squeak. Adults make loud bursts of sound that rhinos far away can hear. But you would not hear them! The loudest sound a black rhino makes is below the range of human hearing.

White rhinoceroses make huffing sounds that scientists can hear only with special machines. But other rhinos can hear them, even over large distances. Scientists say the sounds are similar to the low noises elephants make.

Bird Buddies

Rhinoceroses in Africa have special feathered friends. Oxpeckers, which are also called tick birds, sit on a rhino's back and eat ticks off the rhino's skin. A rhino knows danger may be near if the bird calls out or suddenly flies away.

Chapter 4
What Rhinoceroses Eat

The white rhinoceros is sometimes called the square-lipped rhinoceros because of the shape of its mouth.

Made for Mega-Meals

Rhinoceroses only eat plants, but they eat a lot of them! Rhinoceroses chew up to to 110 pounds of plants a day.

The flexible necks and long heads of rhinos help them reach leaves on trees and tall bushes. White rhinoceroses have a small bump behind their head that is made of super-strong muscles. The bump aids them in raising and lowering their big heads as they eat!

All rhinoceroses have special teeth on the sides of their mouth for crushing and chewing plants. Black and white rhinos have no front teeth. An adult rhino has between 24 and 34 teeth.

The white rhinoceros's mouth has large lips with a wide, square-shaped upper lip. The shape lets the rhino get its mouth low to the ground and clip off whole patches of short grasses, the main food source on the African plains. The white rhinoceros's name comes from the Afrikaans (Dutch African) word *wijd*, which means "wide" and describes the rhino's mouth. English speakers thought the word was "white."

Big Eater

The rhinoceros is the world's largest grazing animal.

Fighting Fangs

Indian, Javan, and Sumatran rhinos have long, tusk-like front teeth. They use them for eating and fighting.

Food for Rhinos

What rhinoceroses eat depends on where they live. Black and white rhinoceroses live in Africa, mainly on grasslands and in areas with bushes and trees. The black rhinoceroses has a flexible, pointed upper lip. Black rhinoceroses use their pointy lip like a hook, helping them to grab and eat branches and leaves. White rhinoceroses eat grasses.

The Javan rhinoceros live in the rain forests of Asia. It eats leaves, young plants, and twigs. It bends young trees and branches with fruit so far down that they break off for a nice meal. The Sumatran rhinoceros lives in the rain forest and on wooded mountain slopes. Its favorite foods are bamboo, figs, and mangoes.

Indian rhinoceroses live in swampy areas surrounded by thick patches of grass. Their lips fold to one side so they can easily tear grass and plants out of the ground.

Water Works

Rhinoceroses need to drink water often to replace what they lose when they sweat and urinate.

The upper lip of a black rhinoceros is pointed, which lets the rhino grab tall plants and pull them into its mouth.

Chapter 5
Rhinoceroses in the World

Where Rhinos Live

ASIA

Nepal

India

Vietnam

Malaysia

Sumatra

Java

AFRICA

Sudan

Dem. Rep. of Congo

Uganda

Kenya

Rwanda

Tanzania

Zambia

Malawi

Mozambique

Namibia

Zimbabwe

Botswana

Swaziland

South Africa

The **dark green** areas show where black rhinoceroses live.

The **blue** areas show where white rhinoceroses live.

The **pink** areas show where both white and black rhinoceroses live.

The **purple** area shows where Indian rhinoceroses live.

The **red** areas show where Javan rhinoceroses live.

The **light green** areas show where Sumatran rhinoceroses live.

Past and Present

At one time in the rhinoceros's 40 million years on Earth, there were more than 30 kinds of rhinos living in North America, Europe, Africa, and Asia. People began to hunt them for sport and for their horns. Today, there are only five kinds of rhinos. Three kinds live in Asia, and two kinds live in Africa.

White and black rhinos live in Africa. They both live in flat lands among many grasses and plants.

The Sumatran, Indian, and Javan rhinos live in Asia. The Sumatran rhino lives in tropical rain forests and along wooded mountain slopes in Sumatra, Borneo, and Malaysia. Indian rhinos live in Nepal and northeast India. Javan rhinos live on the jungle island of Java and in other parts of Southeast Asia.

Most rhinos live in national parks on reserves. These land areas are set up by governments and groups of people to protect the rhinos in their natural habitat.

Rhino Populations

White Rhinos: 11,330
Black Rhinos: 3,610
Indian Rhinos: 2,500
Sumatran Rhinos: 300
Javan Rhinos: 60

Rhinoceroses in Danger

Most rhinoceros species are in danger of becoming extinct. People have been killing these giant creatures for millions of years. Recently people have taken over their land to build farms and cut down trees in rain forests. This makes it hard for rhinos to find food or homes.

People also hunt rhinoceroses for their horns, which can be sold for high prices. Some people believe the horns can help fight illnesses. They grind the horns and add them to medicines. Others use the horns to make knife handles.

Fast Facts About White Rhinoceroses

Scientific name	*Ceratotherium simum*
Class	Mammalia
Order	Perissodactyla
Size	Up to 14 feet long
Weight	Up to 6,000 pounds
Life span	30-45 years
Habitat	Grasslands and woodlands
Speed	30 miles per hour in bursts

It is now illegal to hunt
rhinos and sell their horns,
but some people still do it.
They are called poachers.

Glossary of Wild Words

ancestor an animal from whom others are descended

calf a baby rhino

dung solid waste product excreted from an animal's body

endangered species a species (a specific type) of animal or plant in danger of extinction

extinct no longer living

flexible easily movable

fossil the remains or outline of a plant or animal that has been saved in the earth

grazing eating small amounts of grass or other plants throughout the day

habitat the natural environment where an animal or plant lives

illegal against the laws of a place

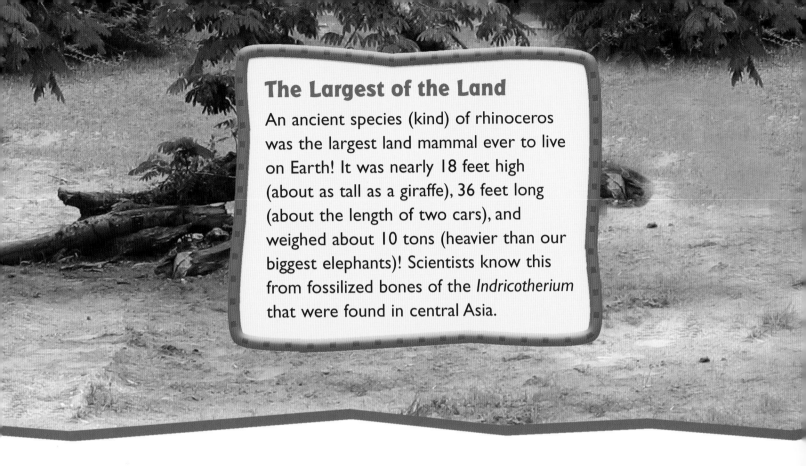

The Largest of the Land

An ancient species (kind) of rhinoceros was the largest land mammal ever to live on Earth! It was nearly 18 feet high (about as tall as a giraffe), 36 feet long (about the length of two cars), and weighed about 10 tons (heavier than our biggest elephants)! Scientists know this from fossilized bones of the *Indricotherium* that were found in central Asia.

mammal	an animal with a backbone and hair on its body that drinks milk from its mother when it is born	**species**	a group of plants or animals that are the same in many ways
mew	to make a cooing sound	**stiff**	strong or hard to move
poacher	a person who kills or captures wild animals where it is against the law	**territory**	an area of land that an animal considers to be its own and will fight to defend
predator	an animal that hunts and eats other animals to survive	**urine**	a yellow liquid containing water and waste products that flows out of an animal's body
		wallow	to roll around in a lazy way

Index